Great Earth Science Projects™

Hands-on Projects About

Saving the Earth's Resources

Krista West

The Rosen Publishing Group's
PowerKids Press™
New York

Some of the projects in this book were designed for a child to do together with an adult.

Published in 2002 by The Rosen Publishing Group, Inc.
29 East 21st Street, New York, NY 10010

First Edition

Book Design: Michael de Guzman

Project Editors: Jennifer Landau, Jason Moring, Jennifer Quasha

Photo Credits: p. 4 © Digital Vision; pp. 6, 7, 16, 17, 18, 19, 20, 21 by Adriana Skura; pp. 8, 9, 10, 11, 12, 13, 14, 15 by Cindy Reiman.

West, Krista.
Hands-on projects about saving the earth's resources / Krista West.
    p. cm. — (Great earth science projects)
Includes bibliographical references (p.   ).
ISBN 0-8239-5847-7 (lib. bdg.)
1. Conservation of natural resources—Study and teaching—Activity
programs. [1. Conservation of natural resources. 2. Science projects.]
I. Title. II. Series.
S940 .W37 2002
363.7'0071—dc21

2001000172

Manufactured in the United States of America

Contents

Saving the Earth's Resources

A **resource** is a supply of energy, a useful material, or a special location. Some energy resources are sunlight, oil from underground, or electricity. Material resources are things like metals that are extracted from the earth, and trees that are cut down for wood. Some locations on Earth are also considered resources, such as oceans and deserts. As the number of people living on Earth goes up, we use more and more of the planet's resources. Some resources, like sunlight, are **renewable**. A renewable resource is one that will not run out. Other resources, like oil, are **nonrenewable**. A nonrenewable resource is one that cannot be replaced in our lifetimes. In this book, you will learn how to save some of the resources you use and protect those that are in danger.

Trees and rivers are renewable resources, but only if people protect them and use them carefully.

Count Your Trash

Most people throw away 5 or 6 pounds (2.3 or 2.7 kg) of garbage every day. That's almost 2,000 pounds (907 kg) of trash in one year, about the weight of three baby elephants combined! Most of what's in your trash is made with resource materials taken from Earth. How many of Earth's resources do you throw away in a day? This project will help you study what's in your garbage. Once you know what's in there, you can take steps to reduce the amount of Earth's resources that you throw away.

You will need
• A pencil or pen
• Paper
• Two garbage bags
• A scale
• Garbage

1 List the following items on a piece of paper: newspaper, paper or cardboard, plastic, aluminum (cans or foil), glass, metal, and wood. Leave a few lines blank in case you want to add something to the list later.

2 Pick a day when you can collect all the garbage you throw away. Put all the dry trash, like packaging and paper, in one bag. Put all the food scraps and wet trash in another bag.

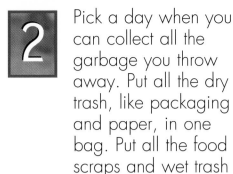

3 At the end of the day, weigh each bag on a scale and add the weights together. Are you above or below what most people throw away? Which bag is heavier? Most of the weight in people's garbage comes from the packaging.

 4 Go through the bag of dry trash and write each item on your list. If you can't decide which category a piece of garbage should go in, make a new category for it. From where is the bulk of your trash coming? Are there ways you could cut down on the amount of that item you use to save Earth's resources?

Set Up a Recycling Center

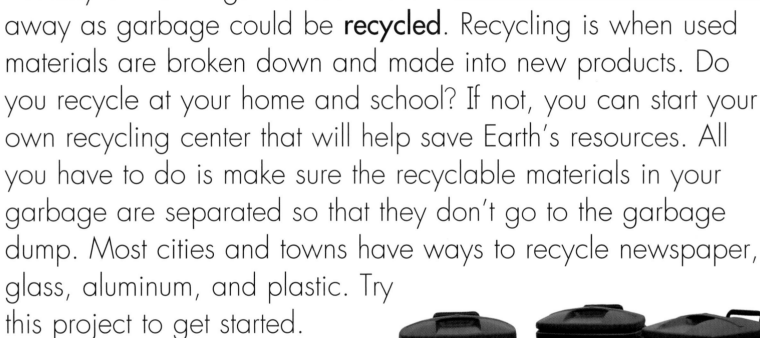

Many of the things that we throw away as garbage could be **recycled**. Recycling is when used materials are broken down and made into new products. Do you recycle at your home and school? If not, you can start your own recycling center that will help save Earth's resources. All you have to do is make sure the recyclable materials in your garbage are separated so that they don't go to the garbage dump. Most cities and towns have ways to recycle newspaper, glass, aluminum, and plastic. Try this project to get started.

You will need

- 3 empty trash cans, large garbage bags, or other sturdy containers
- 3 pieces of construction paper
- Clear tape
- A felt-tip marker
- Garbage

1 Find out how garbage is recycled in your neighborhood. If it's like most places, they probably divide the recyclable materials into three groups: paper/cardboard, aluminum/glass, and plastic. Write each group on a piece of paper.

2 Tape one piece of paper to each container. These will be your recycling bins.

3 Ask an adult if you can pick through the garbage can to pull out the recyclable things. Carefully remove all the paper products and put them in the paper bin. Remove the aluminum and glass and put them in their bin. Do the same thing with the plastic garbage.

4 The next time you throw something away, decide in which bin it goes. Does it go in the garbage can or one of the recycling bins? Encourage your family members to recycle, too. If you don't recycle at school, ask your teacher about how to get a recycling program started at school.

Start a Compost Pile

Part of our garbage is made up of **organic** things, or things made from plants and animals. Food scraps and grass clippings are both organic garbage. We can help recycle these types of resources by **composting**. Composting makes organic garbage into **fertilizer**, a type of food for plants. This way, the resources in your garbage get used again instead of being wasted. Fruit and vegetable scraps, tea bags, old flowers, and even torn-up newspapers all can be composted. You can ask an adult to help you start a compost pile in your own backyard.

You will need

- A space in the backyard (about the size of a bathtub)
- 4 large rocks
- A shovel
- Some soil
- Water
- A ruler
- Organic garbage

Find a place in your backyard where an adult says it's okay to start a compost pile. Put one rock on each corner of the space where the compost pile will be. The rocks will help you keep the pile the right size.

 Separate the organic garbage from the rest in your trash. Make a layer of garbage on the ground between the rocks. The layer should be no higher than 4 inches (10 cm).

 Cover the layer with a shovelful of soil and sprinkle with some water to make it damp. The soil and the water help bacteria and worms to break down the garbage.

Every day add your organic garbage to the pile and make a layer of soil and water. Use a shovel to turn the pile every two weeks. After three to six months, you should have fertilizer that can be used on plants in your yard.

Watch Your Water

Freshwater is one of Earth's most valuable resources. In some places, the freshwater comes from snow or rain that has fallen into rivers. In other places, the freshwater comes from natural underground storage areas made of rock, called **water tables**. Rivers are renewable sources of water as long as there is rain and the rain and rivers are clean. Water tables are nonrenewable. To protect this resource, it makes sense to use only as much water as you need. Many people don't think about how much water they use. Do you? You can start to think about it by doing this simple project. Ask your family members to help, too.

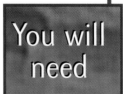

You will need
- Notebook paper (the amount needed depends on the house)
- Pencils (the number needed depends on the house)
- Clear tape

1 Tape a piece of notebook paper to the wall next to each toilet, shower, bathtub, and sink in your home. Tape another piece next to the washing machine. Write the name of each location on the piece of paper and leave a pencil nearby in each room.

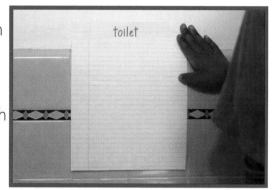

2 Every time you or someone in your family uses one of these things, make a mark on the piece of paper. For example, every time you take a shower, mark the paper next to the shower. Every time you brush your teeth, mark the paper next to the sink.

3 Ask your family to keep track for one week of how often they use each source of water, then look at the results together.

See Biodiversity in Your Backyard

Biodiversity is the number of different types of living things that are found in a particular location. Biodiversity is high when there are many different types of things living in one location. High biodiversity means that an **ecosystem** is healthy. Biodiversity can be protected by saving locations on Earth that have high biodiversity, such as rain forests, coral reefs, and some areas of the desert. You can explore the biodiversity in small locations in your own backyard. See what sorts of creatures you can find. Is biodiversity high or low where you live?

You will need

- A notebook or sketchbook
- A pencil
- A magnifying glass
- A short stick

1 Look in your backyard for large rocks or trees on the ground. If you can't find any, ask an adult to take you to a park or other wooded area. Find a good rock or log and gently flip it over.

2 Look closely at what you see under the rock or log. Are there any bugs or worms? If not you might want to wait for a rainy day and try again. If you see some things, use your magnifying glass to get a closer look.

3 Use a short stick to stir up the soil under the rock. Does anything new crawl or wriggle to the surface? In your notebook, draw the animals you see under the rock or log, then carefully place the object back where you found it. The environment under the rock or log is one example of a special location that provides a home to certain types of plants and animals.

Catch Air Pollution

Earth's **atmosphere** is made up of layers of air and gas surrounding the planet. The air is a valuable resource to humans and animals because we breathe it to stay alive. Sometimes, though, the air becomes **polluted**. Air pollution happens when too many things enter the air at once and build up. Chemicals, dust, and smoke all pollute the air. Many types of air pollution are very hard to measure because they are hard to see. You can do this simple experiment in your room at home to see the air pollution.

You will need

- Four 3 x 5 inch (8 x 13 cm) index cards
- One jar of petroleum jelly
- A butter knife or plastic knife
- 4 zip-seal sandwich bags
- A vacuum cleaner
- A dust rag

16

1 Use the knife to spread some petroleum jelly on two 3 x 5 inch (8 x 13 cm) index cards. The jelly doesn't need to be thick, but it should cover the card entirely.

2 Place one of the cards under your bed or on a place on the floor of your room where it won't be in the way. Place the other card on your desk or another hard surface. Leave the cards there for two days.

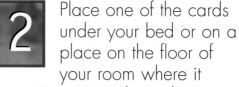

3 Check the cards. There will probably be dust from the air trapped in the jelly. Does one have more than the other? Place each card in a zip-seal bag and save them.

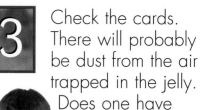

4 Vacuum and dust your room and try the experiment again with the other two cards. What happens this time? Compare the two new cards to the ones you used before cleaning. Is there less dust in the air after cleaning your room?

Clean Up an Oil Spill

The oceans are a valuable resource on Earth. Animals and plants living in the oceans are also resources for humans. If people are not careful, oceans and their populations can be harmed by human activities. **Oil spills** can kill entire populations of ocean animals. Oil spills are very hard to clean up because it's difficult to separate the oil from the water. One way to do it is to **absorb**, or suck up, the oil. Try it for yourself to see how difficult it is, then imagine having to clean up hundreds of miles of oil in the ocean! Wouldn't it be better to stop oil spills from happening in the first place?

- A medium-size bowl
- 1 cup (237 ml) yellow vegetable oil
- 4 cups (1 l) water
- Cheesecloth or gauze
- Cotton balls
- Something made of polypropylene (Read the labels of long underwear, exercise clothes, or jackets to find something made of polypropylene.)

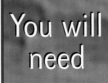

You will need

1 Put 4 cups (1 l) of water in a bowl. Pour in 1 cup (237 ml) of yellow vegetable oil. What happens to the oil and water? You should be able to see the oil and water separate into two layers.

2 Dip the cheesecloth or gauze into the bowl and try to soak up the oil. Does it work? It probably won't pick up much oil, but it will absorb a lot of valuable water. This is not a good way to clean up an oil spill.

3 Dip cotton balls into the bowl and try to soak up the oil. This time you may get a little more oil, but the cotton balls will still absorb a lot of water. This isn't a very good way to clean up an oil spill, either.

4 Dip the polypropylene into the bowl and try to soak up the oil. What happens this time? Oil and polypropylene are made of the same types of chemicals, so they stick together. The polypropylene should pick up a lot of oil and leave the water. Clean-up crews use polypropylene materials to remove oil from the oceans.

Make a Windmill

We use many of Earth's resources to make electricity. Some people use electricity created by coal that has been dug out of the earth. The coal is burned to make electricity. Coal is a nonrenewable source of electricity. There are ways to make electricity using renewable sources of energy. Energy from the sun and the wind, for example, can be caught and turned into electricity. These resources are not used by many people because they depend on the weather in the area. Scientists are working to make energy from the sun and wind easier to use. You can do this project to see wind energy in action.

You will need

- An 8 x 8 inch (20 x 20 cm) piece of heavy construction paper or posterboard
- A ruler
- A pencil
- A pair of scissors
- A thumbtack
- A ¼-inch (6-mm) wooden dowel, about 2 feet (61 cm) long

1 Use a ruler to draw an X on the piece of paper. Make your X by laying the ruler down so that it passes through opposite corners on the piece of paper. Use the pencil to draw a line. Do the same for the other two corners.

2 At the center of the X, draw a 1 x 1 inch (2.5 x 2.5 cm) square. The center of the X also should be the center of the square.

3 Starting at one corner, cut along the pencil line until you reach the square. Do the same for the other three corners. Be sure to stop cutting when you reach the square so the piece of paper stays together. You should have four triangles.

4 Bend the left-hand corner of each triangle into the center, but do not fold down the paper. Use a thumbtack to hold down the corners at the center, and stick the windmill to the wooden dowel. Take your windmill outside on a windy day and watch it spin. The energy from the wind turns the blades and makes the windmill spin!

The Importance of Saving the Earth's Resources

Earth's resources help us create electricity, package our food, and provide homes for animals and plants. Without these resources, Earth would be a very different place to live. We need to protect our resources so that people living in the future will be able to have them, too. As the population of our planet grows, it is becoming harder and harder to protect and save Earth's resources. You can make a difference. Start by paying attention to the amount of resources you use, and then try to cut back or recycle. The projects in this book will get you off to a good start!

Glossary

absorb (uhb-ZORB) To suck up.

atmosphere (AT-muh-sfeer) The layers of air and gas surrounding Earth.

biodiversity (by-oh-dih-VER-sih-tee) The number of different types of living things that are found in a particular location on Earth.

composting (KOM-pohst-ing) A way of making organic garbage into fertilizer.

ecosystem (EE-koh-sis-tum) The way that plants and animals live in nature and form basic units of the environment.

fertilizer (FUR-til-eye-zer) Food for plants.

nonrenewable (non-ree-NOO-uh-buhl) Not able to be replaced once it is used up.

oil spills (OYL SPIHLZ) When large amounts of oil are accidentally dumped in the ocean.

organic (or-GA-nik) Things made from plants or animals.

polluted (puh-LOOT-ed) When human-made waste has harmed the environment.

recycled (ree-SY-kuhld) When used materials have been broken down and made into new products.

renewable (ree-NOO-uh-buhl) Able to be replaced once it is used up.

resource (REE-sors) A supply of energy, a useful material, or a valuable location.

water tables (WAH-ter TAY-buhlz) Natural storage areas for water made from rock.

Index

Web Sites

For more information about saving Earth's resources, check out these Web sites:
www.earth2kids.org/
www.nwf.org/kids/
www.worldwildlife.org/fun/kids.cfm